AF248647

Counting the Lost

Poems by

Gail Peck

Main Street Rag Publishing Company
Charlotte, North Carolina

Cover art: James Peck
Author photo by: James Peck

Special Thanks

I want to thank my wonderful poetry group, and all who've given me encouragement in the writing of this book. My gratitude to the Vermont Studio Center where many of these poems were written. My deepest gratitude to my husband, Jimmy, for his love and support.

Gail Peck

Library of Congress Control Number: 2011935284

ISBN: 978-1-59948-317-7

Produced in the United States of America

Main Street Rag
PO Box 690100
Charlotte, NC 28227
www.MainStreetRag.com

ACKNOWLEDGMENTS

Grateful acknowledgment is made to the following journals in which some of the poems appeared, sometimes in different versions:

Aires: "Collage," "Ring Around the Rosie," "Canada"
Blackbird: "Refuge," "The Men"
Cave Wall: "Inside," "Forbidden Fruit," "Portrait of the Sea," "The Tree,"
     "Through the Gate to Madgeburg Barracks"
Dos Passos Review: "Children in the Park," "The Parents"
Ekphrasis: "Russian Beggarwoman II"
Interpoezia: "Angel of Death," "A Song," "In the Fürherbunker,"
     "Nightfall in the Camp," "The Autobiography of Rudolph Hoess,"
     "Transport"
Iodine: "Abstract"
LiturgicalCredo: "Lullaby," "One, for Praise," "Prams at Auschwitz,"
     "Rest," "Woman Reflecting," "The Goblets"
Main Street Rag: "Checking for Lice," "House at Terezin,"
     "In Berlin, 1957-1960"
Nimrod: "Gabi and Josef," "Dwellings at Terezin,"
     "Embroidery on Paper" (finalists for the Pablo Neruda Prize),
     "The Visionary" (semi-finalist for the Pablo Neruda Prize)
Persimmon Tree: "Fountain with Six Children"
Prism: "Starlight in Dark Room," "Sketch of a Child's Hand," "Black and
     White Photograph of Hungarian Jews"
roger, an art and literary magazine: "Seed for the Planting Must Not be
     Ground," "Lamentation for Ernst Barlach who Died in 1938"
Unmovable Feast: "Funeral," "Hiding," "Pieta," "Tower of Mothers"

Anthologies:

Charlotte Writers Club: *Journey Without*: "Oktoberfest"
Kakalak 2007: "Still Life," "Woman with Dead Child"
Kakalak 2008: "Old Woman"

The poems in section II appeared in the chapbook, *From Terezin* (Pudding House Publications, 2008).

For all those who have perished in war, especially the children

CONTENTS

I

II

III

To stand bravely erect deserves in itself neither praise nor admiration; its worth depends on the grievous difficulty which has made it necessary.

—Ernst Barlach

THE GOBLETS

Rubble from bombs still in the city
as we rode to Brandenburg Gate
where my parents, my sister and I
stood looking up at those majestic horses.
If someone had offered to take a snapshot
we would have moved closer, my stepfather,
1ˢᵗ Sgt. James B. Pruitt, mother holding
my baby sister, Joni, and Sherry next to me,
smiling a lie of happy togetherness in that
place divided between West and East.

Mother, who grew up poor and longed
for pretty things, sent the maid
to the East Sector to buy crystal
goblets with money she'd saved, and the maid
brought them, one by one—deep burgundy
and cobalt blue—to our side of Berlin,
now a thing of beauty on a shelf. No one
drank wine, so their heft was never felt.

They came back with us to the states,
and we packed them for every move.
Six of them given to me as a gift when I married.
I don't use them as I prefer to see the clarity
of wine, and worry about the lead.
But, I'll keep them. I should tell my children
about these goblets etched in history.
My mother, sitting at the table in front
of the lighted china cabinet, playing cards,
laughing and smoking with her friends, Kitty and Helga.

THE VISIONARY

after Ernst Barlach, relief,
Hamburg Memorial, 1931

A woman in profile looking
not at us but to the future,
her daughter's head against
her breast. Their dresses
press together, and they wear
no shoes. There is nowhere to go.

What she sees now
isn't the hunger of the first war,
women in line for bread while
husbands, fathers fight in the trenches.

She sees bombs that will fall
on Hamburg. Streets and canals
on fire, people who've fallen asleep
from the fumes, others stumbling
over charred corpses, and there's
that boy in the distance behind
his mother whose clothes
have caught fire. He's smothering
the flames with his hands.

SEED FOR THE PLANTING MUST NOT BE GROUND

after Käthe Kollwitz, drawing

Her arms are shelter, her body.
Every birth was a wake of pain
until they were lifted from her, washed
and placed on her breast to nurse.
She touched fingers and toes.

Older now, they are playing with
a wooden wagon, a ball, while she ladles
soup into bowls, trying to scoop
a bit of potato in each.

Hans spills his, and she wants to cry—
instead, takes spoonfuls from the other portions.
She will never let these boys go to war.
Look at Berlin, windows with nothing behind.

Come see the hunger of six eyes,
hear the begging of stomachs.
Once there was an apple she cut
into threes, telling the boys to chew slowly.

The war goes on—who can rest?
Peter, Herman, Hans, almost numb
to the constant sirens and explosions,
want to stay in their beds and sleep.
Count them and count them, the numberless sheep.

RUSSIAN BEGGARWOMAN II

after Ernst Barlach, bronze sculpture

She sits with one arm extended, hand cupped
for whatever might be placed there.
Her covered head rests on her skirt.
She curves into beauty not defined by her face
we can't see—graceful fingers that in a different life
might play the piano, flute. She is the essence
of silence, but must have sat on a busy street,
brown shoes and black passing by.
Did she get used to being ignored?
During the hours rung by bells
did she think of a child to feed? I, too,
might have spurned this woman in the flesh,
forgetting my grandmother who once knocked
on doors in the countryside where she lived—
houses left unpainted with wood stacked on porches—
asking for food not for herself but my mother
whose boots were held together with safety pins.
Someone filled a shoebox full, enough
for them both, and they sat on the cold ground
and divided the bread, the meat, the sweetness of cake.

WOMAN REFLECTING
after Käthe Kollwitz, drawing

Where are my children now,
my right son and my left son
as they called themselves.
One killed in the first war,
the other still fighting
while snow falls in Berlin.
The church bells have been melted down
for ammunition, and the New Year, 1916,
will steal quietly in.
Smell of the Christmas fir in the corner,
each sad ornament reclaiming its shape
when hung from the boughs,
and the cake she made with rations of flour,
the last of the cinnamon, ginger.
When they were small they stood by her side
while she creamed butter and eggs.
Don't run or the cake will fall, she'd tell them.
She'd pluck a straw from the top of the broom
for testing. Tomorrow she'll return to sketching—
the face, the hands, they are what speak to her—
a woman sitting, one large hand
covering half her face.

WOMAN WITH DEAD CHILD

after Käthe Kollwitz, etching

Death has made them both naked.
The mother is sitting, holding her child,
her mouth and chin pressed against the child's chest
so that we see only the lines in her forehead
and her closed eyes.
The infant I carried six months
lived through the night. When I asked
to see her, I was told to wait until morning.
Then I had to give a name to what was only spirit,
and she had to be buried
since she weighed more than a pound.
It was wrong of them not to let me see her,
wrong of me to wait months before going
to stand over the marker in the Louisiana sun.
The day comes back to me now,
and how months later,
I found, in a folder, a certificate
my husband had put there--
the smallest of prints:
curve of the right foot, curve of the left.

BLACK AND WHITE PHOTOGRAPH OF HUNGARIAN JEWS

after a photograph from
The Holocaust Chronicle

She bears the weight of grandmothers,
stooped in a checkered jacket and kerchief,
clutching a bundle, the smallest
grandchild beside her, possibly three,
head uncovered, holds her sister's right hand.
In the left, the sister has a small white bag.
The tallest girl follows,
hands in pockets, legs bare—
one foot firm on the ground,
the other with only heel touching.
The oldest girls have identical coats,
belted in back, decorated with a button.
They are walking along a railroad track
at Auschwitz, beside an electrical fence
that keeps even the birds away.
No face is visible, nor can we see
those who walk in front or behind.
I hear young voices—*How much farther?*
Where are we going? Will Mother be there?
Their mother must have bought the coats,
new shoes that sent the girls running
to their papa, all shouting at once, *See?*

OLD WOMAN

*after Robert Capa, photograph
of a refugee in Barcelona, 1939*

sitting on a low stone
bench wearing a skullcap
under a scarf, one hand cupped
over a handkerchief, you
don't have a suitcase,
just an open tattered box
that holds a blanket with a memento
on top, and your eyes don't say
what the lines in your
hands do: kneading bread,
hanging clothes to dry,
lifting the heavy iron of a past
that will follow you and your
shadow, long skirt in motion,
your possessions held
so the extra warmth won't spill
this January day that's taking
you to wherever you are going.

HIDING

A compilation of voices of children
who were hidden in Holland

I went into my little box.
For the second time that day
my heart stopped. I heard
knocking on the door, loud voices.

I thought, this is it—
inside my little box
gray clouds that might
be a German coming
to get me, knocking.

A man came upstairs,
and he looked around.
You didn't dare move—
everybody would hear you.
The loud voices knocking.

. . . might be coming
to get me. I was barefoot.
I managed to escape
into a meadow and was there
all day, my heart knocking.

Gray clouds, dark. Flat
Dutch land. Loud voices
on the horizon coming
to get me. A meadow,
my little box. Don't move.

REFUGE

*after Robert Capa, photograph
taken near Wesel, Germany, 1945.*

Such boredom, the mother with her chin resting
on her clasped hands, the boy with part of his face
covered, cap pulled down, his elbow on the earth
outside the hole they are crouched in
while there's fighting in the distance. The small girl
with blonde hair, a barrette holding part of it back,
is the one who intrigues me. Unlike her peasant mother,
she is pretty and wears a coat. I can see
a hand peeking from a sleeve. She could be
the age of Eva, the daughter in *Sophie's Choice*,
the child who was carried away screaming,
clutching a bear and a flute. Sophie in line
at the concentration camp, finally answering
the command, saying, *Take my little girl.*

If the woman in Capa's photograph had to throw
her body over one of her children, which would it be?
Sophie letting her lover, Nathan, piss on her, break her ribs.
That number on Sophie's arm, offering herself
to the Commandant in attempt to save her son.
To choose between your son and daughter. I am looking
at the girl standing in the trench turned toward her mother.

TWO ASLEEP

after Ernst Barlach, wood relief

As if after making love,
this man and woman peaceful,
now clothed, maybe dreaming
of a child taking shape,
a boy with his father's nose,
his mother's chin,
and how when the child
is able to walk he'll stand
by their bed telling them
to open their eyes, and
he'll run the wheels
of a small toy truck
over the side table,
and they will want always
to protect him, removing
sharp objects, warning him
only to go knee deep
in the ocean, but their dream
will turn fearful when
they look away and he steps
deeper, far from outstretched arms.

MANIA HALEF

after a photograph from
        The Holocaust Chronicle

With those bangs and watchful eyes,
she looks like a doll, standing in a sunsuit,
wearing anklets, slippers, and holding
a smaller doll. I am trying to guess
the color of the satin ribbon
in her hair—I can tell it's satin
by the sheen. When she is seven
she'll be killed at Babi Yar, one of 33,771 Jews.
I don't know what she was wearing
that September day before they told her
to strip and lie in a ravine, or if her parents
whispered her name, or if when it was over
she lay, as the caption states some did,
on the body of her mother.

ANGEL OF DEATH

is what Joseph Mengele
is called because he
greets you at the camp,
and points you left to live,
or right to die, and spends
his whole day doing it.

He is gleeful when twins arrive,
subjects for his experiments,
and places them in a special
barrack. Once he ordered doctors
to stitch two together.

Come closer to Uncle Mengele—
one of the twins steps forward—
big black boots and piercing
eyes as two toffees are placed
into a hand. *Are you warm
enough? Do you have
enough to eat?* Then the brother
is called, and he also gets two candies.

For now, their only fear is not to be
together. They are each other's
shadow, growing larger, smaller.

PRAMS AT AUSCHWITZ

One hundred hundred wheels
brought from all the city streets—
Warsaw, Krakow, Lodz . . .
Satin linings now wet with snow
hold no cry, no lullaby or rattles.
Tops that opened and closed.
Here come some more
with shiny chrome
pushed into the store room.
Outside the crematorium,
a checkered one with fringe
turned over in the mud.
Wind sometimes sets those
upside down wheels spinning.

NIGHTFALL IN THE CAMP

A blessing and a curse
for those who slept so close
together because of space
and warmth. Forbidden to huddle near
the one inadequate stove.
But the cold was easy compared
to dreams where there's only present,
and food abundant—look at the table
set with candles, fine silver holding
sweetmeats, cakes. Oh, dreams
were the worst is what they said,
the constant talk of food—
a rat in the stomach gnawing,
a rat that can't escape. Bring day
and labor, slip into those too big
shoes stuffed with paper. Take your bowl
you don't lose sight of—no spoon—
to stand in line. The dreams that made you whole
vanish with falling snow that covers
earth, and somewhere beyond
the roofs of houses where children slowly wake.

CANADA

Canada, they called it,
the store of confiscated
goods of those deported,
land of plenty.

Shoes in piles, leggings,
coats, mountain
of toothbrushes.
The kapos had their pick,

but others had to barter
their piece of bread.
Everyone wished
for something warm—

no need for handbags.
They wanted soap,
a few dreamed
paper and pen.

Whose offering,
this candle flame
hidden in dark night
to celebrate a child's birthday?

And the miracle of sardines
torn in silvery pieces
pinched between fingertips
of those who shared.

PIETÁ

after Käthe Kollwitz, bronze sculpture

The child seems too large
for the mother's lap, his long legs
bent at the knees over her skirt.
Her face is downcast,
and one hand touches his.
Her other hand covers her chin
as if in thought.

Perhaps this is Kollwitz holding
her son the way she once held him
as she sat on the floor sketching
in front of a mirror, and when she groaned,
he said, *Don't worry, Mother,*
it will be beautiful, too.

Is this how she brings him back,
Peter, fallen in the first war—
> *Last night I dreamed once more that*
> *I had a baby . . . I would go on always*
> *holding it in my arms . . . I would*
> *not have to give it away.*

His head on her chest, body unclothed
so that she is his warmth.
You want to run your hand over
the scarf on the mother's head.

LAMENTATION: IN MEMORY OF
ERNST BARLACH, WHO DIED IN 1938

after Käthe Kollwitz, bronze sculpture

Before others arrived
she entered his studio
where his casket waited.
His small dog ran around it, sniffing,
and above, the mask
of the Güstrow angel.
He'd refused to be buried
in Güstrow Cathedral
where the Nazis had taken down
his bronze angel to melt.

They had come to her home,
peered into her studio.
From then on she would carry
a vial of poison.

Some things they could never take.
Not the grace that drives
one over and again
to the work table to shape faces
that evoke silence but are not silence.

FUNERAL

after Robert Capa, photograph, Naples, 1943

Many would be beautiful without grief.
These mothers, most with their mouths
open in a cry revealing uneven teeth.
Some with handkerchiefs—one
is wiping her right eye, another
covers her lips. The white linen glows
against black dresses.
Their boys had stolen guns
and ammunition to fight the Germans.
A woman at the center displays
a photograph of her son. He is
a shadow next to her face.
The woman nearby has her hair pulled back,
an earring catching light, the only adornment
other than a wedding band.
Capa said these images of mothers
were his truest victory. This man
who couldn't bear taking pictures
of camps where relatives had died.
Years later he stood outside
Auschwitz and photographed the fence.

TOWER OF MOTHERS

after Käthe Kollwitz, bronze sculpture, 1938,
and two photographs in Newsweek, 2006

Today their hearts are stone,
these mothers who've created
a fortress with their bodies,
their children peeking from the folds
of skirts. One mother has her bare feet
planted, another has her fist in the air.
No, they shout at marching boots,
planes overhead. Nothing can get
to the children now—what kind
of game is this they ask?
It has no name.

*

In the photograph of the gravesite,
a girl in blue pants and green top
is behind a casket. She is not
looking at it, her eyes are clouds.
She leans against a woman's lap,
her head tilted away
from the soldier who cups her chin.
The girl has a hand full
of red flowers, the other held loosely
around one rose about to fall.

*

The boy, probably four, lies face
down on dirt, rock. His pants
shredded by a mortar, his feet, legs, arms
soiled from dust. White shirt someone
must have buttoned, one sleeve
not fully covering the arm bent backward.
Who will come gather him, wash
his body, comb his hair?

II

WHAT WE SAW AT TEREZIN, A HOLDING CAMP FOR JEWS

A white cell with one tiny barred
window at the top. *The Gate of Death*
we walked through. A pocked wall
where even after the Germans surrendered,
prisoners were lined up and shot.

Laundry drying on a line
strung across a courtyard
in the Main Fortress.

One room, as life had been,
roped off at the museum.
Numbered bunks, numbered
suitcases stacked high.

Children's paintings, drawings,
collage. Ela painted
the sun with lips slightly open
and eyes sealed shut.

AT TEREZIN

Fragments from Terezin

In Terezin in the so-called park

the heaviest wheel rolls across our foreheads

Every eye shines with fixed waiting
and for the word *when*

Our good friend Time
sucked each figure empty

We got used to sleeping without a bed

Somewhere far away out there, childhood sweetly sleeps

Here the sound of shouting, cries,
And oh, so many flies

That bit of filth in dirty walls,
And all around barbed wire

The sun goes down
and everything is silent,
only at the guards' post
are heavy footfalls heard

But in the ghetto, darkness, too, is kind
to weary eyes that all day long
have had to watch

And mothers bend their heads into their hands

One branch after another
is snatched by fire

The nearing storm rouses me,
it makes me want to shake the world

Ten o'clock strikes suddenly,
. . . they toss and turn . . .
Finally, one by one, they grow silent

CHILDREN IN THE PARK

*after artwork by Gabriela Freiova and Petr Holzbauer,
children at Terezin Concentration Camp*

This drawing on yellow paper
depicts a park that could be any park
except it's not. Children play beneath
the trees sprouting cabbage leaves.
One child poised in front of another
holds what might be a present,
a box decorated in art class.
This is what Gabriela left behind.

Two boys and a girl stare out,
jump ropes suspended over their heads.
The girl has dots for eyes like all the others,
but it's the arch of her eyebrows
that makes her seem so lost
within herself. On the right,
several boys dressed alike walk in file,
and seem oblivious to this park
created for the Red Cross visit.

Overnight, street signs appeared,
curtains at some windows.
These children know
this cannot last, and do not smile.
That patch of flowers
beneath a tree, no one can pick.
Nor can they leapfrog over one another,
or sail paper airplanes above paths
covered with new sand.

Soon there will be nowhere to sit,
benches removed, trees
bare, snow covering it all.
But, the trains keep arriving,
like the one Petr sketched on paper,
hurrying along the track beside a river
he scribbled his name in.

CHECKING FOR LICE

after artwork by Helga Weissova,
a child at Terezin Concentration Camp

Mother is sitting in a chair
while the doctor leans over
with a magnifying glass.
He's bald and has a black mustache,
his colorless coat below his knees.
Again, tonight, we'll sleep in misery,
without Papa who was taken to another camp,
carrying his clothes in a sack.
Will they shave Mother's head,
will she wear a kerchief,
grow thin and be like the rest,
lost in her simple dress
with the Star of David on the left,
a brooch of yellow, puckered cloth.
The doctor stands in his good shoes,
color of chestnuts that grew
near the house with a backyard fence
where roses bloomed so fragrant.

HOUSE AT TEREZIN

after artwork by Hana Kohnova,
a child at Terezin Concentration Camp

Square eyes and arched-mouth doorway,
it sits in a dark patch of green
edged by a field.
A red pointed hat, the roof,
like those worn at parties
where there's cake and games to play.
The roof peaks into an area
left unpainted—the same white
as the windows, door.
The small house seems abandoned,
but smoke escapes from the chimney
where it touches mountains almost black.
Above those, a bit of grey—the sky
you could get to if you could fly high enough.
If only there were a bird
those two sloped curves children draw,
a tree or sun. Who does the fire
warm in this house
without a walkway, road or path
to lead you in or out.

ABSTRACT

after artwork by Nely Silvinova,
a child at Terezin Concentration Camp

Of course it's the sun,
though so much like an eye
with darker red at the center.
It hovers between
streaks of yellow across
the top and bottom of the cover
of this sketchbook Nely may have
been allowed to keep, carrying the sun
through all the seasons.
Her name in huge black letters,
and the mark over each i
has furred to insects,
something she used to find disgusting.
It's lice she dreads,
having her long hair cut.
She lives in House 14, group V—
everything has a number,
and she paints 1944—
two years separated from her mother
who used to yell up the stairs
to hurry while she soaked and played
in the big bathtub, light
coming through the window near the ceiling,
the sun carving a pond onto the floor,
so that she could hop from water to water.
Now, a small cup carried carefully
to dip this brush in,
lavender cloud, swirl of white.

GABI AND JOSEF

after artwork by Gabriela Freiova,
a child at Terezin Concentration Camp

I drew myself, my pigtails tied with ribbons, and my brother
Josef beside me. I could have drawn the sun, the dead man
lying on a cart, but I didn't. My blouse is white, Josef's shirt
is yellow, and we're standing in the grass. We don't have many
clothes, and what we have stay in suitcases marked with our
names. In this picture I colored, we're not doing anything.
Maybe we're wishing we could walk home, to our house with
lots of rooms. Josef left his puppet. He'd pull the strings and
make up stories. Everyone calls me Gabi, so that's how I sign
my name. You can't get lost here. You can only go so far. How
I want to go home. I dream all the time of sitting at dinner in
the rickety chair Papa never got around to fixing, eating all I
want. He says we'll return soon, but it's been two years. People
keep leaving. I think they're going to another camp. Marie's
father was taken away, and she worries her mother will go too.
Marie draws beautiful pictures and paints flowers that look real.
I could start over, add a tree or building. Somehow I like it just
like it is. Me and Josef, holding hands.

SKETCH OF A CHILD'S HAND

after artwork by Frantisek Brozan,
a child at Terezin Concentration Camp

Hand that drew
picked up stones
held a cup   a spoon   a fork   a knife

Give me your hand
his mother said   his papa said
when he was pulling away

Rubbed the fur of the dog's back
velvet ears   snout to tail
Fetch the ball   Fetch the ball   (rubbery   slobbery   ball)

Fist to smash a flea

Palm scraped on wire
Aching finger where the bee stung

Hand saying hello   goodbye
Inside the pocket of a sweater   rusted coin
to save or give away

FORBIDDEN FRUIT

after artwork by Eva Heska,
a child at Terezin Concentration Camp

Today the children are playing "Roll Call"
and "Block Leader." One boy falls in the snow
pretending "Sick." He lies there a minute,
socks poking from worn shoes.
Some gather stones and begin
to build a chimney. When it's time for art class,
Eva draws "Paradise," her pencil sketching
long-stemmed apples circling a tree,
a pear tree, heavy coconuts on a palm.
Why not a tree with everything,
even cherries, bananas. Animals
reside below—cat, rabbit, turtle.
Birds fly toward a sun that's partly visible—
half a mouth and an eye.
Staring straight ahead, two figures—
masked doll-face and rag-doll standing.
Seen from the back, a naked girl reaches upward,
about to snap an apple from its branch.
The snake who's done his work crawls away.

STILL LIFE

after artwork by Marie Fantlova,
a child at Terezin Concentration Camp

Marie is painting a water pitcher
blue as her name, curving the brush
for the large handle, now so big on the page
it threatens to tip the small base.
The flowers, too, will be blue, except for some
with petals that seem to float in space.
Her mother loved this pitcher, and it's better
than painting fruit which they never have,
although there's an orchard outside this building
where the girls live. No not food,
though the grownups seem happy exchanging recipes
when there's only lentil soup made from powder,
week after week. She'll paint flowers
like the ones she used to pick while her brother
ran with a net catching butterflies—there seemed
to be so many, what could it matter? Oh, where
have they taken Irena? All she has to remember
her by is a drawing on office paper. Tonight
she'll hold Dora's hand until they escape to dreams.
Let them be good, not Dora crying *Wolf, Wolf.* Let them be
of someone arranging cornflowers, poppies, tulips
in a blue pitcher on a green table against a yellow wall.

STUDY OF LEAVES

after artwork by Milan Biennenfeld,
a child at Terezin Concentration Camp

Black leaves on long stems
Each lying in a shadow
Lifeless to the wind

EMBROIDERY ON PAPER

after artwork by Dorit Weiserova,
a child at Terezin Concentrtion Camp

I make a bouquet for my mother.
She lives in another house.
I cried when they said I was now too old
to stay with her. Most of the girls here
are nice, and they gave me yarn
to sew over what I'd drawn on an office form.
I start with a basket, sew it black,
and stretch light blue to the bottom,
and to make it seem woven,
tie that down with orange French knots.
One flower is red, one is black,
one, light blue, and the same blue
for another flower with only two petals
because I've decided to put
a yellow bee there.
Flowers are what I do best.
Satin stitch would have been pretty
for the centers. It takes more yarn,
so I paint them. Erika says
the drooping one looks like a lady bug.
She's always saying things like that,
she wants to be the best in everything.
There's enough green left over
for one small leaf,
and I'll make a blossom peeking out.
Twice I've pricked my finger—
no one has a thimble.
Mother had several at home.
I can't wait to show her this.

PORTRAIT OF THE SEA

after artwork by Ruth Gutmannova,
a child at Terezin Concentration Camp

Red-orange coral,
little black sea horse, his eye
taking it all in, watchful of the jellyfish.
Two starfish float above him.
Shrimp live here, too,
in the aqua swaying grass.
Is that a human figure, faded black,
pants ballooned, floating at the edge,
hovering above the ocean floor.
A sea snake goes to investigate,
headed west like the others.
Death's so constant here,
the clown fish isn't interested.
Immune to the poisonous anemones,
he has no fear and turns
to swim in the opposite direction.

INSIDE

after artwork by Vilem T. Eisner,
a child at Terezin Concentration Camp

With thick strokes
Vilém outlined everything
in black. Four small boys
on a bench have their backs to us,
facing two bunk beds.
Signed at the bottom,
V.T. Eisner,
the *T* like a bird
that might land on the top pallet
near the window where
a lone cloud peeks through.

School is forbidden, but perhaps
one child reads to another,
a story of someone lost on an island,
something they've seen on maps.
For this moment, they may imagine
being surrounded by water,
not close enough to swim to anything.
And which of them has held
a shell to his ear, listening to the drifting sea?

When a guard walks in,
they'll jump up quickly,
hide the book beneath a pillow,
move closer to the stove that eats the coal.

RING AROUND THE ROSIE

after artwork by Anita Spitzova,
a child at Terezin Concentration Camp

Six girls in a circle holding hands
The four faces you can see
have lifeless eyes

A pocket full of posies
Ashes ashes
We all fall down

Their skirts scrape the ground

Anita Erika Marie Gabi Eva Ruth
stepping clockwise into time
that has turned the grass green
but will bring the snow
the sound of shovels
and bitter bitter cold

SNOW AND ICE

artist unknown,
a child at Terezin Concentration Camp

How brightly they're dressed
in green and blue
mittens, hats, scarves.
Some sled down the hill,
one skis, others skate.
Red lips all, from cold,
and more snow swirling.
It's too much fun to go inside,
although feet are getting numb.
    Turning in a circle on skates
    without falling . . .
    Is that Mother calling?
Here snow becomes ice.
This was before, in the village
of the baker, old clockmaker,
the store with hard candy, butterscotch
to savor, turning it with your tongue,
making it last.

THE TREE

artist unknown,
a child at Terezin Concentration Camp

You draw a Christmas tree with a cross on top,
candles on each branch, presents marked
with names. Orange floor, urn of flowers,
window pane of sun. You draw yourself
looking at the tree, wishing
for a dollhouse, book or skates.

   How slow the days,
   and then the night's long hours
   until first light, smell of coffee,
   sound of feet. The stocking
   of fruit and nuts—which box to open first,
   big or small?

Now, Anita's peeking over, asking
about the tree, won't it catch fire,
how many presents do you get?

Then before you can stop her,
she takes your red crayon
and colors a bow in your yellow hair.

COLLAGE

after artwork by Ruth Gutmannova,
a child at Terezin Concentration Camp

The sun, not entirely round,
    dances atop
a mountain, its many arms
    and legs on fire.
To the right, a cloud
    shaped like a mouth
threatens to spoil the show.

Backdrop of mountain peaks
    casting shadows
against an aqua sky.
    Another cloud,
a violin,
    hums the music
for this sun that

just goes on
    and will not take a bow.
This is the sun shining
    on Prague—the roof of the house
called home, the linden trees,
    the path beneath,
the old dog left behind.

DWELLINGS IN TEREZIN

*after artwork by Josef Novak,
a child at Terezin Concentration Camp*

It is a bunk, not a bed
with soft mattress, where
each night I lie and smell the wood
frame. Beneath is my suitcase
that has clothes, and a picture
of my papa I keep. I try to be
still while others sleep toes to toes.
There are no curtains,
and when I'm awake
I watch for the moon. Papa says
it's a promise, the coming and going
and filling out, that even in all its changes,
it stays. During the night I sometimes
climb down and go from window
to window stepping softly,
afraid I might scare the moon away.

STARLIGHT IN DARK ROOM

after artwork by Sona Spitzova,
a child at Terezin Concentration Camp

A round table, gooseneck lamp,
a chair, a stool. No one moving
the chair or adjusting the lamp,
no voice at this stage
where the curtain has risen,
and the window watches for someone
to walk to it and make a wish
on the yellow stars caught
in the half-moon's glare.

THROUGH THE GATE TO
MAGDEBURG BARRACKS

*after artwork by Eva Wollsteinova,
a child at Terezin Concentration Camp*

First go to F 111 where pencils and paper
are smuggled in. One boy writes awhile,
hands the pencil to the boy next to him
who writes an equation for math, hands the pencil back.

You walk on to the hospital where Dasa and Jana
lie feverish with typhoid, hair matted to their heads.
Best friends swearing never to part.
Nearby, a young boy helps a blind man walk,
asks if he can call him Grandpa.

L 318, where it's now dark,
the door open, whispers of transports.
Yellow slips of paper held near the candlelight.
Marking of clothes and suitcases.

Another day begins and you're still here,
more talk of the Red Army closing in.
You see children who've been ordered
to help pass along cartons of ashes
to be thrown in the river.
Some fall open. Pieces of bone.

You want to go now, be anywhere but here.
Then a tank comes rumbling, shaking the ground.
Everyone shouts and cries.

The years pass, and you stand again
where it all happened, where three young girls
sit in the grass, one holding a rabbit,
warm, live creature the other two reach to pet.

IN THE FÜHRERBUNKER

They were playing "Red Roses
Bring You Happiness" on the Victrola.
Eva Braun, now Eva Hitler, drinking
champagne. Berlin, above, in shambles.
Albert Speer's vision blown apart.
A matter of hours, and the poison
already tested on Hitler's beloved
dog, Blondi—*Here girl,*
here. In the end, he himself

didn't trust it and also squeezed
the trigger, Eva found slumped against him.
Magda Goebbels so distraught she'd forgotten
to feed her children—she would feed them
later as they slept sedated in their bunk beds: one,
two, three, four, five—one more ampoule

to crush between the teeth,
and only this oldest child apparently
struggled against the poison,
bruises on her face. None
of them found until days later,
under white sheets, lying
there on down pillows, each
of their names beginning with an H.

BERLIN FAMILY

after Margaret Bourke-White, photograph, 1945

The only motion we sense is the woman
holding a blanket, white as angel wings,
about to cover her two children. Her head is bowed
in this room with pattern on pattern—a cloth over
the table, floral print chair, but it's the carpet
you're drawn to. A boy and girl lie upon it, their heads
wrapped in gauze. Behind a table
there's a large portrait propped against the wall and,
on the table, a plate with something stacked so high all
that shows are eyes witnessing this. When
the mother takes her own life, will she
leave this room? How did Bourke-White
get this shot? Did the mother agree? Many
imitating Josef and Magda Goebbels who killed
their six children and then themselves.
These two with small hands the mother has lifted
and placed across their waists.

TRANSPORT

*Photograph of a woman in Berlin
after a bombing raid, 1942*

Half human, half monster, wearing
   a gas mask, pushing a baby carriage
hurriedly past a movie marquee

where part of a word—L O R I A
   is visible through smoke. She's like
the figure from the movie, "The Fly,"

that I saw in Berlin when I was eleven,
   an army brat afraid of getting lost,
but lonely enough to go out.

A scientist experiments with a transport machine,
   and decides to enter it himself,
not knowing a fly has flown in. The man

emerges with the arm and head of a fly,
   and the fly has escaped
with a small human head and arm.

The fly must be found. The white carriage
   is rolling along, the baby inside
 might have its own mask made

like a body suit, but air needs pumping in.
   Hurry, hurry. An infant longing
for its mother's face, a mother

playing peek-a-boo, disappearing
    only briefly then returning
with a smile. The wife tells her son

to try and catch the white fly
    he's seen, and screams
when she finds the maid with a swatter.

Hadn't she told her husband how frightened
    she was: *Electronics, rockets, earth satellites,*
supersonic flight, everything going so fast. All

his reassurance that life as we know it
    will change, and humanity will never fear again.
The huge black head of the husband

when the wife pulled the cover off wasn't as scary
    as the close-up of the fly, its human face
and fat tongue shrieking, *Help me, Help me.*

DUTCH ORPHAN

after Robert Capa, photograph, 1945

Parentless, nameless,
the stork dropped you.
How harrowing your flight
as wind beat against
your blanket that was never
warm enough. Left there
beneath a tree where you
were found. So little food,
but you've grown, and someone's
slipped a gown of printed leaves
over your head. Someone's even
brushed that fuzz of hair.
You stand with one hand curled
over the crib's bar,
the other held out.

AMBULANCE DRIVERS

*after Robert Capa, photograph taken
near Cassino, Italy, 1943*

A break in the work day.
Two female drivers in uniform

are knitting. One sits on the
running board, the other

on the littered ground, a ball
of yarn next to her. Their boots

are muddy, and although it's December
they don't seem cold. Maybe

they are knitting a blanket,
or a sweater to wear during days off

when they might put on
dresses or skirts, paint lines down

the backs of their legs since there
are no stockings, dab lipstick

on their cheeks to rub in for rouge,
then go dancing or to sing in a club

where they could stay all night, forgetting
the wails of ambulance 8695F,

the chained wheels rushing
over the rough terrain.

THE PARENTS

after Käthe Kollwitz, woodcut

Now that their child is dead
they have become one body.
Grief brings them to their knees,
each holding the other's weight.
The husband has covered his face
while the other hand is held loosely
at his wife's side. Her face is against
his arm—his sleeve wet
from her tears. We can't see her hands
which lie in the folds of his coat.
Long ago these hands caressed one another
in passion, and now must find their way
back to the tasks of the day—
cutting bread, pouring milk. But to eat without appetite
in a house familiar and strange. Plums,
easily bruised, in a bowl on a table
where the three of them sat.
The clock on the wall encasing time,
the cuckoo's call now too shrill.

WOMAN WITH SHAVED HEAD

after Robert Capa, photograph,
France, 1944

A policeman pushing you
with his billy club. He will not strike
as you hold this child, fathered
by a German. You cannot stop no matter

if the baby cries and cries—look only
at the dark hair that won't lie down.
How long will it take your hair to grow back.
Get a scarf, tie it at the chin, because they'll wait
for you outside their doors, turn away

from you who tasted foreign words while
the rest went hungry. Don't you deserve
women laughing, children staring, men too old
to fight, wearing berets, spitting at your feet.

THE AUTOBIOGRAPHY OF RUDOLF HOESS: COMMANDANT OF AUSCHWITZ

(Found poem)

*Although I became accustomed to all that
was unalterable in the camps, I never grew
indifferent to human suffering.*

I have never personally hated the Jews.

*By command of the Reichsfhurer SS
the doctors were to dispose
of the sick and especially the children,
as inconspicuously as possible.*

A short, almost smothered cry and it was over.

*Many of the women hid their babies among
the piles of clothing. The women believed
that the disinfectant might be bad for their
smaller children, hence their efforts to conceal them.*

. . . and the doors were screwed shut.

*. . . Jehovah's Witnesses . . . They stubbornly
refused to do work that had any
connection with the war.*

*I put all my ability and will into my work;
I lived for it entirely*

Let the public continue to regard me
as the blood-thirsty beast, the cruel
sadist and the mass murderer, for the masses
could never imagine the commandant
of Auschwitz in any other light.

I am concerned no longer about my personal
fate, but only about that of my wife and children,
for what will happen to them?

THE MEN

after Margaret Bourke-White's photograph,
The Living Dead of Buchenwald, *1945,*
and an anonymous snapshot

They don't want you to see them this way,
in their striped uniforms with whatever
coat they could find. Four of them
have a hand curled over barbed wire—
one whose belt hangs from his waist, one
wearing what looks like a woman's jacket.
An older man leans on a cane, a patch with numbers
on his pants. The man at the far edge has large hands
and high cheek bones, and is obscured slightly
by wire that's eye-level. Buchenwald, named
for the surrounding beech forests—Beechwood, excellent
for fires and making smoky German beer.

In a snapshot someone took, German soldiers
are gathered around a table, set amid trees,
lifting their beer mugs for a toast. One soldier
has his arm thrown over his buddy,
all of them smiling. The location could have
been Buchenwald, a labor camp where
many were worked to death, where
the entrance gate was carved with the words:
Jedem das Seine—To Each His Own.

The Hungarian Stephen Casey was at this camp.
After liberation he returned to the ghetto
where he'd lived. No one recognized him.
Then his dog, a fox terrier, came sniffing, jumping.
I became myself again, he said. Some returned to the cold

of Russia, the warmth of Spain, countries stretched
between, all carrying a common language in their eyes.
Back home to where—until there became
too many—ashes of dead prisoners were sent
in sheet metal boxes, *Postage Due*.

ALCHEMY

Cherub candlestick, one leg crossing
the other, white porcelain with
pink and yellow roses—petals
that could chip in all these moves.
My mother bought you when
we lived in Germany, ten years
after the war. Made in Dresden,
a city where Augustus the Strong had ruled,
and believed in alchemy (it was the Age of Reason).
He needed gold due to all he'd spent on wars,
brought Johann Friedrich Böttger to sit above
Meissen and boil and burn and batter
combinations of lead and mercury to no avail.
Instead, his eureka was porcelain,
setting the factories in motion.

When Dresden was bombed, the factories
would come tumbling down. Hard to believe
anyone survived when looking at that famous photograph,
the life-size sculpture Güte—The Goodness—
angelic figure in profile, still intact,
shoulders bent slightly forward, folds
of a robe draped to the tip of one hand,
the palm upward—*We had no way to surrender.*

Who could live civilized again, listening to Wagner,
setting the table with gold-rimmed china, serving demitasse
cups after dinner, pouring from a floral chocolate pot?
You escaped, little fat-butt cupid with dreamy eyes,
your mouth locked forever over a flute.

OKTOBERFEST

The carnival of carnivals.
Pull a lever on a slot machine and you might
win marks; throw balls at pins—if you knock down
enough, the huge, stuffed bear could be yours.
My luck that day seemed only in being
away from my stepfather, growling,
baring his teeth. What would he do to my sisters?
I had mother's sole attention, although
she wouldn't let me see the four-armed man.
How can a woman crawl in a box that's sawed through,
and come out whole? In the bier garten
under linden trees, I was eating bratwurst
with spicy mustard. People on benches swayed
to music, drinking ale from steins.
We were miles from our quarters on Flanaganstrasse
where I'd held Werner down until he cried
Uncle. 1958, no one thinking of running
to shelters with blankets, carrying their children,
yelling, *Schnell, Schnell.* Rudolph Hess, Hitler's Deputy,
was in Spandau Prison. Oom-Pah-Pah. Oom-Pah-Pah.
Hunger seemed far away. It was as if there'd never
been a war, would never be one again.

CHILDREN OUTSIDE

*after Zippy Orlin, photograph of
Displaced Persons, Bergen-Belsen*

Has the sun ever felt this good?
These children lying on their stomachs,
pushing back with their hands,
stretching. With eyes closed
they can't see what is home for now.
The girls wear no tops, but big bows
decorate their hair. A low fence made
of branches divides the field. They could
jump over it, but are not used
to being unruly, not used to play.

Now stand up, hold hands,
form a circle, no not a straight line.
Turning and turning in the clover
where later you can search for
a four-leaf. Whoever finds one
can press it between paper.
It will be yours.

IN BERLIN, 1957-1960

We'd flown across an ocean
to meet my stepfather we hadn't seen
in months. At the hotel, my sister and I
under a feather comforter that kept sliding off,
the baby in a crib, and there at the foot
of the big bed, my mother's underwear.

Cokes cooled in a window box, and we'd
go out to walk in snow and buy gummy bears,
the smallest bears ever, and I'd eat them
one by one: red, orange, green.

We'd live for awhile over a bar,
a sign out front with a bear on hind legs,
breathing fire, something about to go up in flames.

Where's my boots, my goddam belt, my stepfather
yelled, and mother's mice feet scurried to find them.
Go out and play, she told me. Kids were bouncing
a ball against a wall, but I knew nothing of their
language except eins, zwei, drei. Later, I'd go
to American school where I'd refuse to learn
the guttural sounds. Where the boys
drew Swastikas on their desks.

Once in quarters my sister and I had our own room,
and there were rooms in the basement for maids,
but none stayed there. They came and went,
affordable even for a sergeant's pay.
We were issued china with the name Rosenthal
on the back, and had to pay for whatever we broke.

Dear Diary, I wrote, I miss home.　Yesterday
the M.P.s took my stepfather off in handcuffs,
because he was drunk and turned the furniture
upside down, but he's back now since
his commander told Mother he's a model soldier.
No one but us saw him crossed-legged on the floor
holding up addition and subtraction cards for my sister—
a thump with his big thumb for each wrong answer.

I threatened to jump off the third story balcony.
Go ahead, Mother said.　After every argument,
a time of peace, a trip to the zoo where the bombed
buildings stood, history I didn't understand,
or the German woman I bumped against
saying with disgust, *Americans.*　We lived in a city
where a dividing Wall would be built after we left.

What would I remember?　Riding in a tank,
sleeping on a train to Frankfurt, sitting beside
the window of the plane, watching all below
get smaller until the clouds made everything invisible.

ONE, FOR PRAISE

In the photograph I've framed
he's with his company,
standing in Berlin's snow,
everyone wearing a beret.
It was what he did best,
this chain-of-command.

And years later while in Vietnam
he was incensed to know
our flag was being burned in U.S. streets,
worn as a patch on blue jeans.

He lied about his age
to join up—the 101st Airborne,
Screaming Eagles, worked his way
to Sergeant's stripes, and led us three girls
onto fields where jets flew over.
Yes Sir, we answered at attention
knowing not to question.
When finally he sat in the V.A. Hospital
in that locked unit for people who
don't know where they are,
we could speak our piece.
He nodded while that caged parrot
in the waiting area said, *Hello, Hello*,
and sparrows came to the window's ledge.

My sister Joni was crying so hard at the funeral,
the elderly veteran placed the folded flag
onto her lap. I pointed to our mother—
Anyone can make mistakes, he said.

The salute of guns in the distance
startled us. I was thinking how once
my stepfather told me he became
a paratrooper for the extra pay,
and how he must have felt that first time in the plane
watching the line get shorter,
until it was his turn to stand in the doorway,
then step out.

REST

after Käthe Kollwitz, Rest in the
Peace of His Hands, *relief for a grave*

As close as I'll get to the past—this face tilted,
eyes closed, one small hand clutching a shroud—
reminding me of you. I thought I wanted to be there
when you were dying, the nurse saying
on the phone your son ran from the room
refusing to sign you over to the next world,
and your past lover telling me, *It isn't pretty,*
what's happened to your sister. Later I'd call
the morgue in Florida, and all they'd say is your body
was there, and no one would return my calls.
I'd already seen what alcohol had done,
an image in the mirror you wouldn't own up to.
When you were small and we lived in Germany
you'd come frightened to my bed, restless, arms and legs
thrown over me. I'd dream of a crushing weight.
It was there that my stepfather, your real father,
first lashed his belt against your six-year-old body.
Afterward I'd pull on your boots and jacket, take you
out in the snow. The rest of your life you'd live
where it was warm, never needing a coat.
Now, what does it matter that I don't know
if your ashes were ever strewn over your garden?
I can only return you to beauty.

FOUNTAIN WITH SIX CHILDREN

after Robert Capa, photograph,
Stalingrad, 1947

Ghostly, these marble children
on a pedestal, holding hands,
circling an alligator whose jaws
I can't see. They must have
been singing a song when bombs
fell. Stairways leading nowhere
in the background. How
did this fountain remain intact,
this large funny frog
with eyes atop its head
looking straight at me,
other frogs spaced
an equal distance apart?
If I knew Russian I would sing,
and these children would kick
up their heels and dance.
There's only a trickle of water left,
so the frogs can't jump
in, and nowhere for my
wishful coin to sink. A woman
sits on a park bench facing
the fountain. She wears a scarf
in the August heat, and is waiting
for her barefooted daughter,
the one dancing in the swirling skirt.

STEFFA HASSON

*after Zippy Orlin, photograph,
Displaced Persons*

Here at Bergen-Belsen where
you live, your doll goes everywhere
you do: to eat, to play, to bed.
She's all you took from the Lvov Ghetto
except some clothes. Doll with
blonde hair, molded like
her body. She cries if someone
else holds her, and when she wets
the bed you scold, because
she's old enough now to know
better. You won't leave her
as you were left. Go to sleep,
you whisper. She can't close
her eyes, and sees the monsters, too,
the ones grownups say aren't there.
But you know how in dreams
they chase and threaten to take
Lidia away and smash her.
You'll never ever give her up.

LULLABY

Wind, wind, a shaking,
wind that keeps awaking . . .

Gone the light of the sun,
now a cradled moon.
Hush and sleep,
dark passes soon.

Wind, wind, a shaking
wind that keeps awaking . . .

Night's a closing of wings,
day is an opening over.
Soon stars will disappear,
throw back their quilted cover.

Wind, wind, a lisp,
wind, wind a whisper . . .

Dawn shines through the window.
The tree outside has stilled,
has shaken all its sorrows.
Wind has had its fill.

A SONG

I'm reading about the Holocaust, how the Jews slowly gave up
everything—first their businesses, their cars, then their pets,
radios, Victrolas, and musical instruments. When I picture a
man turning in his harmonica I think of my friend, Bill, whose
harmonica is like his right hand, one of his doctor hands he
greets patients with, hand feeling for lumps here and there.
On occasion he's even treated those in the office to a tune,
asks them if they have any stories about mules. If you know
Bill, you don't ask why. Neither do you question when he sees
two homeless women in the cold, drives to Starbucks and takes
them coffee. That's him out in the dark looking for the lost cat,
just as he searched in Vietnam for the things he tells us about.
Recently I wrote to him: Sometimes it's the small horrors that
are the worst. Life without music, feet with nothing to dance
to, no clapping hands. Play me a song, Bill.

NOTES

"Hiding" owes a debt to *Beyond Anne Frank: Hidden Children & Postwar Families in Holland*, Diane L. Wolf, University of California Press, 2007.

The poems in Section II were based on *I Never Saw Another Butterfly: Children's Drawings and Poems from Terezin Concentration Camp 1942-1944*, edited by Hana Volackova, Schocken Books, 1993, and also *I have not seen a butterfly around here: children's drawings and poems from Terezin*, edited by Hana Volavkova, The Jewish Museum Prague, 1993. In addition, a great source of information was *Theresienstandt: A Guide*, (Theresienstandt was what the Germans called Terezin) Jehuda Huppert and Hana Drori, Vitalis, 2005. Terezin was a holding camp for Jews, most who later perished at Auschwitz.

"In the Führerbunker" owes a debt to *In Hitler's Bunker: A Boy's Eyewitness Account of the Fuhrer's Last Days*, Armin D. Lehmann and Tim Carroll, The Lyons Press, 2004.

"The Autobiography of Rudolf Hoess, Commandant of Auschwitz" owes a debt to *Commandant of Auschwitz*, Rudolf Hoess, Phoenix Press, 1951.

"Alchemy" owes a debt to *Armageddon in Retrospect*, Kurt Vonnegut, Putnam, 2008; also to *Dresden: Tuesday, February, 1945*, Frederick Taylor, Perennial, 2004.